CO**

Cornwall is a very special county set apart from the rest of the country, not just in a geographical sense but also in its scenery and in the distinctive character and traditions of its people. Its very name conjures up a host of enduring images – of stone cottages tumbling to the sea, seagulls and fishing boats in tiny harbours, heather-clad moorlands punctuated by weird granite tors, glorious beaches with Atlantic rollers sweeping in, the fine prospect of St Michael's Mount (pictured left), spring wild flowers in every hedge and wall. We hope that this book gives you a glimpse of what makes Cornwall such a special place.

Le Comté de Cornouailles est bien particulier, différent du reste du pays, non seulement du point de vue géographique, mais aussi par ses paysages et par le tempérament et les traditions caractéristiques de ses habitants. Son nom même suggère une quantité d'images inoubliables: de petites maisons de pierre qui dévalent vers la mer, de mouettes et de bateaux de pêche dans des ports minuscules, de landes couvertes de bruyère ponctuées d'étranges buttes de granit, de plages magnifiques balayées par les lames de houle de l'Atlantique, du beau panorama du Mont St Michel (illustré à gauche), de fleurs sauvages dans toutes les haies et toutes les murailles au printemps. Nous souhaitons que ce livre vous donne un aperçu de ce qui fait de ce Comté un endroit spécial.

Cornwall unterscheidet sich vom übrigen Teil des Landes nicht nur durch seine geographische Lage, sondern auch durch seine Landschaft sowie die Traditionen und den unverwechselbaren Charakter seiner Menschen. Schon der Name beschwört eine große Anzahl bleibender Bilder herauf: steinerne Häuschen am Meeresrand, Möwen und Fischerboote in winzigen Häfen, Heideland mit seltsamen Granithügeln, herrliche, von atlantischen Brechern umspülte Strände, die schöne Aussicht auf St. Michael's Mount (links) und blumenübersäte Hecken und Mauern. Dieses Buch soll Ihnen einen Einblick in diesen besonderen Ort gewähren.

Land's End

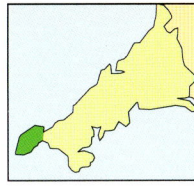

Land's End and Penwith

Mousehole, a popular fishing village.

Mousehole, petit port de pêche en vogue.

Mousehole, ein beliebtes Fischerdorf.

◄
Lanyon Quoit, near Morvah, is over 4,000 years old.

Lanyon Quoit, près de Morvah, a plus de 4.000 ans.

Der über 4.000 Jahre alte Lanyon Quoit, nahe Morvah.

St Ives

▲
Bunker Hill.

▶
St Ives harbour with, inset right, the beach nearby. Inset left is the Tate Gallery, which reflects the town's long association with artists.

Le port de St Ives avec (cartouche droite) la plage voisine. Cartouche gauche: la Tate Gallery, qui reflète la longue association de la ville avec des artistes.

Der Hafen von St. Ives mit dem nahegelegenen Strand (oben rechts). Daneben die Tate-Galerie, die die langjährige Verbindung der Stadt mit Künstlern widerspiegelt.

The Lizard, England's most
southerly point. Inset, the
Lizard lifeboat.

The Lizard, extrémité sud de
l'Angleterre. En cartouche: le
bateau de sauvetage.

Der südlichste Punkt
Englands, "Die Eidechse",
und das örtliche
Rettungsboot.

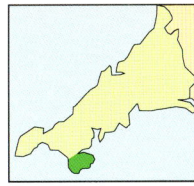

The Lizard

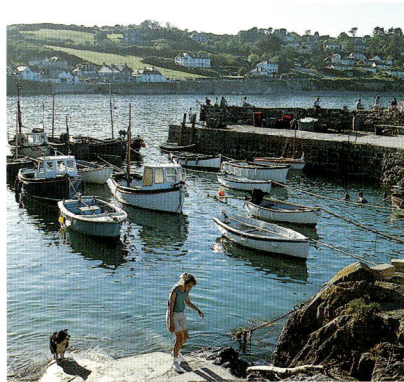

▲ Low tide at Cadgwith Cove.

La marée basse à Cadgwith Cove.

Cadgwith Cove bei Ebbe.

◄ Coverack Cove, once a smuggling village.

Coverack Cove, jadis village de contre-bandiers.

Das einstige Schmugglerdorf, Coverack Cove.

◄ Helston, famous for its Floral Dance.

Helston, célèbre pour sa Danse des Fleurs.

Helston ist bekannt für seinen "Blumentanz".

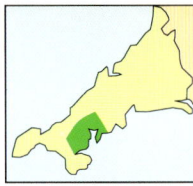

Falmouth and Truro

▲
Falmouth. The old harbour is on the deep estuary of the River Fal. The modern holiday resort is on the sea coast nearby.

Falmouth. Le vieux port, sur le profond estuaire de la Fal. La station balnéaire est tout près, sur la côte.

Falmouth. Der alte Hafen liegt an der tiefen Mündung des Flusses Fal; der moderne Ferienort befindet sich an der nahegelegenen Küste.

▶
St Mawes Castle (16th-century).
Château de St Mawes (XVIᵉ siècle).
St. Mawes Castle (16. Jahrhundert).

Truro Cathedral

Land's End, the most westerly
point in England, with
Longships Lighthouse beyond.

Land's End, extrémité ouest de
l'Angleterre, avec, au large, le
Phare des Longships.

Land's End, der westlichste
Punkt Englands, mit dem
Longships-Leuchtturm im
Hintergrund.

▲
Fowey and its estuary.
Fowey et son estuaire.
Fowey und seine Flußmündung.

◀
The flower Spotted Cranesbill.
Becs-de-grue en fleur.
Der dunkeläugige Storchschnabel.

▶
Mevagissey harbour.
Le port de Mevagissey.
Der Hafen von Mevagissey.

Fowey and Mevagissey

▲ Lanhydrock House.

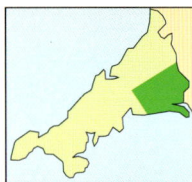

East Cornwall

▶
Cornwall's mild weather produces beautiful flowers.
Le climat doux de la Cornouailles produit de belles fleurs.
Das milde Klima Cornwalls erzeugt wunderschöne Blumen.

▼
A ferry boat and a bridge link East and West Looe.
Un ferry et un pont relient les deux parties de Looe.
Ein Fährschiff und eine Brücke verbinden die beiden Teile
von Looe.

Fishing boats drawn up the
beach at Polperro.

Bateaux de pêche tirés à sec
sur la plage de Polperro.

An Land gezogene
Fischerboote in Polperro.

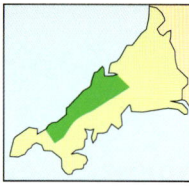

From Hayle to Padstow

▶
Hell's Mouth near Portreath.
Hell's Mouth, près de Portreath.
Der "Höllenschlund" bei Portreath.

▼
The charming fishing port of Padstow on the beautiful estuary of the River Camel.

Le charmant port de pêche de Padstow, sur le bel estuaire de la Camel.

Der malerische Fischereihafen Padstow an der Mündung des Flusses Camel.

Newquay.

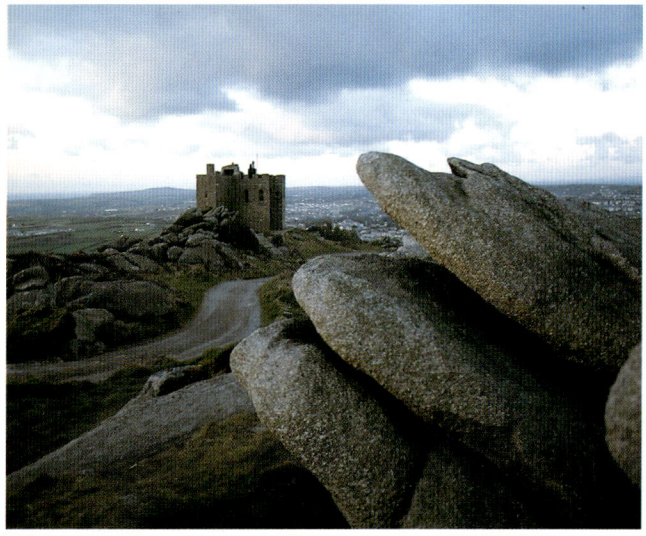

Carn Brea, near Camborne, is a large Iron Age hill fort.

Carn Brea, près de Camborne, est une grande forteresse de l'Age de Fer.

Carn Brea ist eine große eisenzeitliche Hügelfestung bei Camborne.

▲
Jamaica Inn, at
Bolventor, made
famous by Daphne
du Maurier's novel
of the same name.

Jamaica Inn, à
Bolventor, l'"Auberge
de la Jamaïque" du
roman de Daphné
du Maurier.

Das Jamaica Inn,
Bolventor, wurde
durch Daphne du
Mauriers gleich-
namigen Roman
berühmt.

►►
The ruins of Tintagel
Castle, linked in
legend with King
Arthur.

Les ruines du Château
de Tintagel, associé à
la légende du Roi
Arthur.

Die mit der Artussage
verbundene Burgruine
von Tintagel.

►►
Sunset at Bude, a
popular North
Cornwall resort.

Coucher de soleil à
Bude, station balnéaire
populaire de
Cornouailles du Nord.

Ein Sonnenuntergang
am Meer im beliebten
Ferienort Bude.

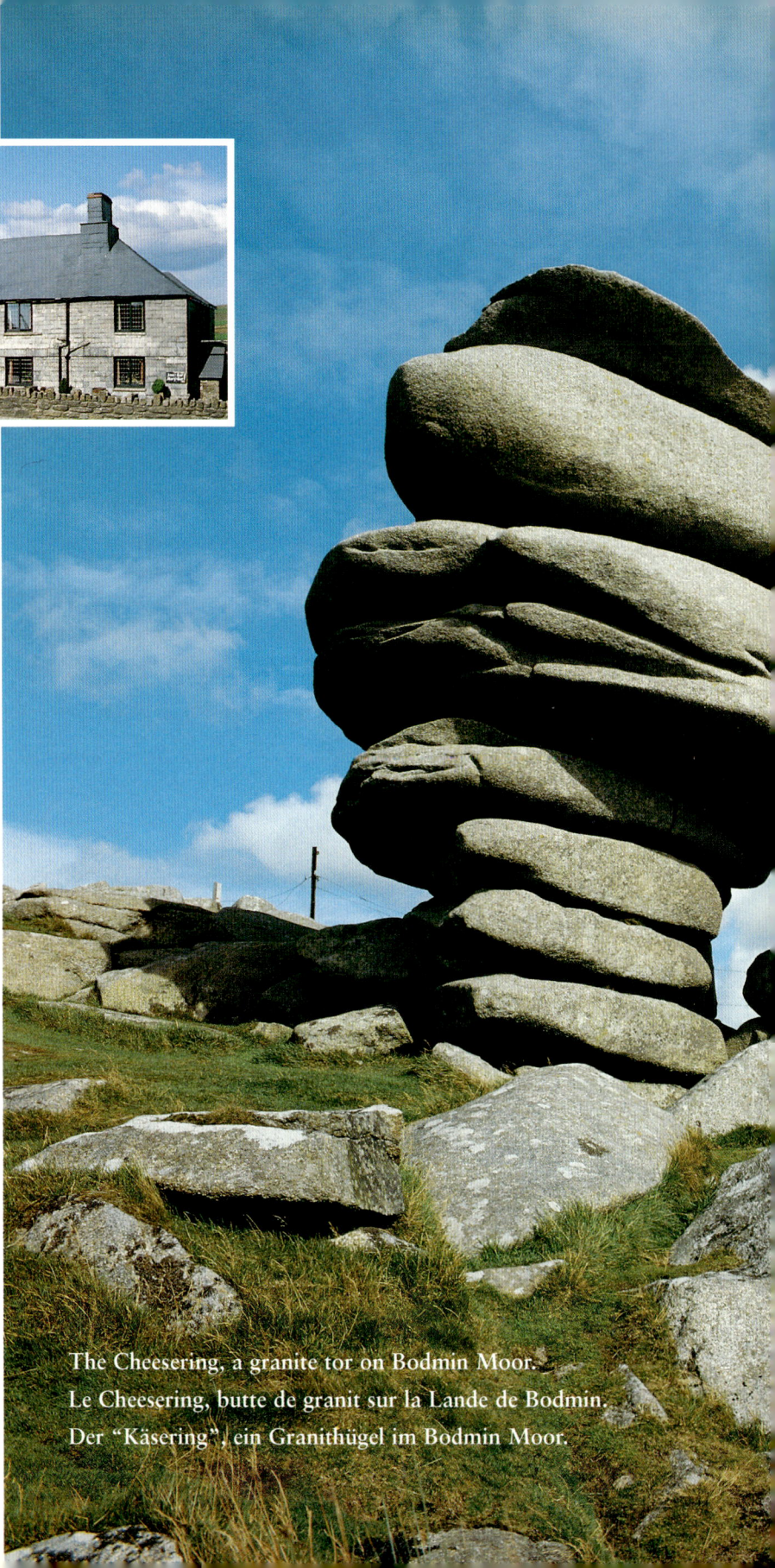

The Cheesering, a granite tor on Bodmin Moor.
Le Cheesering, butte de granit sur la Lande de Bodmin.
Der "Käsering", ein Granithügel im Bodmin Moor.

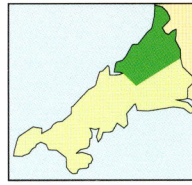

North Cornwall

Land's End.